AFRICA IN PERSPECTIVE

The Russell C. Leffingwell Lectures

The Russell C. Leffingwell Lectures, inaugurated in 1969, were named for a charter member of the Council who served as its President (1944–46) and Chairman of the Board of Directors (1946–53). Mr. Leffingwell was a lawyer in private practice for 18 years, and was subsequently associated with J.P. Morgan & Co., eventually as Chairman (1948–53), and then with the Morgan Guaranty Trust Company.

The Leffingwell Lectures are given periodically at the Council on Foreign Relations. They provide an opportunity for a distinguished non-American to reflect on his or her experience in public life and to address a major international issue from the perspective of that experience. The first Leffingwell Lectures were given by Lester B. Pearson. Subsequent Leffingwell Lecturers were Eduardo Frei Montalva, Alastair Buchan, Guido Carli, Gordon Richardson, Denis Healey, Robert Marjolin, and Valéry Giscard d'Estaing.

The lectures are made possible by the generous support of the Leffingwell family and the Morgan Guaranty Trust Company.

AFRICA IN PERSPECTIVE
MYTHS AND REALITIES

OLUSEGUN OBASANJO

COUNCIL ON FOREIGN RELATIONS

58 East 68th Street, New York, NY 10021

COUNCIL ON FOREIGN RELATIONS BOOKS

The Council on Foreign Relations, Inc., is a nonprofit and nonpartisan organization devoted to promoting improved understanding of international affairs through the free exchange of ideas. The Council does not take any position on questions of foreign policy and has no affiliation with, and receives no funding from, the United States government.

From time to time, books and monographs written by members of the Council's research staff or visiting fellows, or commissioned by the Council, or written by an independent author with critical review contributed by a Council study or working group are published with the designation "Council on Foreign Relations Book." Any book or monograph bearing that designation is, in the judgment of the Committee on Studies of the Council's board of directors, a responsible treatment of a significant international topic worthy of presentation to the public. All statements of fact and expressions of opinion contained in Council books are, however, the sole responsibility of the author.

Library of Congress Cataloging- in-Publication Data

Obasanjo, Olusegun.
    Africa in perspective.

    (The Russell C. Leffingwell Lectures; March 1987)
    1. Africa—Politics and government—1960–.
2. Africa—Economic conditions—1960–. 3. Apartheid.
I. Title. II. Series: Russell C. Leffingwell lectures; 1987.
DT30.5.0225   1987   960'.3   87-15442
ISBN 0-87609-026-9

Contents

Foreword

General Olusegun Obasanjo's important lectures represent a milestone in the Council's Russell C. Leffingwell lecture series given by outstanding foreign statesmen. Nigeria's former head of state, the first African lecturer since the inception of the series in 1969, reflects a new era of leadership as Africa concludes its third decade of political independence. For the first time since the advent of political independence, African states are beginning to realize the benefits of a new breed of senior statesmen fitting the Leffingwell profile—former high officials committed to serving their countries as disinterested counselors rather than active aspirants for power. Although General Obasanjo is young to be classified as an "elder statesman," he and others like him are becoming an invaluable repository of wisdom and experience for their countrymen and neighbors, willing to look with frank and candid eyes at African policies as well as external forces at work on Africa.

In his lectures, General Obasanjo reflects a widespread questioning among black Africans north of the Limpopo River about what three decades of nationhood have brought them, and what possibilities, problems, and changes may lie ahead. This admirable leader has structured his lectures around three sets of issues: (1) the progress, or lack thereof, in political, social, and economic endeavors after more than 25 years of political independence; (2) debt, disarmament, arms sales, and development; and (3) racial conflict in southern Africa. His experience eminently qualifies him to speak about each of these areas.

As Nigeria's head of state between 1976 and 1979, General Obasanjo grappled successfully with the establishment of political institutions suitable to the Nigerian nation, while presiding over a carefully prepared transition from 13 years of military rule to democratic civilian government. Nigeria's largely American-style political system, fashioned in an impressively painstaking constitutional process to suit its African context, was probably more complicated than Nigeria could, at the time, manage or afford, but it went a long way toward resolving many of the basic problems that had impeded national unity since colonial times. General Obasanjo's reflections on the successes and failures of the constitution give us a frank and insightful analysis of political institutions which are consonant both with African traditions and present and future needs. It is noteworthy that General Obasanjo emphasizes that he does *not* believe it "appropriate to advocate one political arrangement or system of government for all African countries."

Turning to the second set of issues—debt, disarmament, arms sales, and development—General Obasanjo discusses these complex and related matters with clarity and perception. In so doing, he demonstrates his mastery of the unique art, given to so few, of making complicated matters simple and understandable to the layman. Especially illuminating and instructive are his analysis of and prescription for sound programs of economic development in sub-Saharan African nations.

In dealing with development, this modern-day Cincinnatus speaks not only as a former soldier and head of state, but also as a devoted practitioner of his current profession—farming. Stressing that the greatest handicap of African leaders "in formulating development policy at the time of independence was their lack of adequate experience and exposure in economic matters," he points out that post-independence economic development programs largely ignored the rural areas "where most of the people were living." Since the independence era began, he says, too many African governments have raided their most basic source of wealth—*agriculture*—to spur what their foreign advisors termed an industrial "takeoff." While paying lip service to the importance of farming, he points out, they in fact discriminated against agriculture so that productivity began to fall off almost everywhere. General Obasanjo's example has manifested to his countrymen in a most personal way the urgent priority of agriculture. Moreover, in the ensuing years, a number of other influential Nigerians have followed suit, creating what may become a potent lobby for a sector that until recently has remained politically weak in most parts of the continent.

On South Africa—the political issue that unites most Africans—General Obasanjo again possesses unique credentials. As the co-chairman of the Eminent Persons Group (EPG), he was mandated by the Commonwealth to explore the possibilities for a settlement within South Africa in 1985 and 1986. Virtually the only modern African leader to have conducted political talks with both blacks and whites within the Republic, he sounded out South Africans of all political persuasions. Astute, receptive, and judicious, he helped to spearhead a process which brought the South African government closer than ever before to the prospect of negotiations with authentic black opposition. Although the Botha government ultimately scuttled this brave endeavor, General Obasanjo emerged as a much-admired and respected leader with an unparalleled understanding of the internal dynamics of the struggle that is rending that troubled nation.

His view of South Africa is shaped by the perception of the necessity for unity. Any hope for a negotiated settlement, in his view, depends both on a united front among blacks within South Africa and on close cooperation among America and its Western allies to put economic pressure on the Botha government. But he also reminds us that the prospect of cooperation is threatened by imposition of superpower conflicts on a regional struggle far removed from global ideological concerns.

The impressive balance and realism he displayed as a leader of the EPG characterizes his approach to each of the separate issues considered in these three lectures. At the same time, his approach to all three is unified by a somewhat visionary theme. In looking at the origins of Africa's political and economic problems, he balances the distortions of colonialism against the shortsightedness and widespread corruption of African leadership. Showing how Western economic behavior and the advice of well-meaning foreign experts has immeasurably increased Africa's problems, he also drives home the need for Africans "to shed their blinders about the essential challenges of economic, social, and political development" and themselves take the lead. He calls for the reexamination of the number of nation-states and divisions arbitrarily created for Africans by outsiders in the nineteenth century. He further suggests that in our ever-shrinking world it is critically important "to cooperate and eventually coalesce in order to have adequate control over changes that are bombarding all of us." Pointing out that many other nations have found they have to work with others in such areas as security, the economy, trade, the environment, and health, he concludes that for Africa such cooperation must be "the new imperative."

While he was head of state, General Obasanjo staunchly backed the idea of West African economic unity as embodied in the problem-ridden Economic Organization of West African States (ECOWAS). Although this experience left him fully aware of the difficulties of such enterprises, he courageously states that he sees no viable future for many African states unless such institutions as ECOWAS become a living reality, and urges African states to surrender some aspects of their sovereignty in order to achieve viability and genuine independence.

In the best tradition of this distinguished lecture series, General Obasanjo has distilled a rich store of experience and reflection into a message of particular current impact. We are grateful to the Leffingwell family, the Morgan Guaranty Trust Company, and the Ford Foundation for providing the impetus and platform which elicited this important contribution.

May 1987

Cyrus R. Vance

ONE

Africa: Myths and Realities in Politics and Governance

There can be no question that these days the world's political, security, and economic situations often have a disproportionate impact on Africa—an impact, sadly, more often negative than positive. The larger contexts of colonialism, East-West rivalry, and the international system of trade and financial arrangements have compounded problems of development and stability for individual countries and the continent alike. After more than twenty-five years of political independence for most African countries, it is appropriate to take stock and assess the progress, or lack of it, in our political, social and economic endeavors.

Many, especially Africans, are tempted to blame Africa's ills on colonialism and the continuing injustice perpetrated by the strong industrialized West against the weak countries of the Third World. I do not, however, intend to indulge in "colonialist-bashing" and "West-bashing," however convenient the explanations such an approach provides for the inadequacies that lie behind our scarcely stellar performance. I must, however, refer to relevant aspects of history and current events to lay a basis for understanding the contemporary situation and some of Africa's deep-rooted problems, for which I will proffer some possible steps toward solutions. Taking the political challenges first, I turn to the myths and realities in African politics and governance.

Africa is a continent that has prompted Africans and non-Africans alike to myth-making, at times unwittingly and at others quite purposefully. One of the most enduring of such myths portrays Africa as a dark continent of wildlife, where very little that is human happens aside from drought, famine, disease, incessant coups, civil wars, social disorder, and corruption. That this view grows from persisting myths which derived long ago from slavery and the slave trade is clear.

Africa has had to face a twentieth-century international system of nation-states of basically European construction. Yet another European global system, the colonialism dating from the nineteenth century, had in most cases destroyed the structures of African political and administrative systems. Whether the colonial powers ruled "indirectly" or supplanted the existing machinery of government, the same result of stifling and eroding the existing culture was achieved. The greatest harm done to the colonial subjects was to undermine their self-confidence, determination, and self-esteem.

World War II and the ideals of the United States of America enunciated by President Franklin D. Roosevelt as he set forth his famous Four Freedoms combined with the nationalistic fervor in the colonies to hasten the process of bringing independence to Africa. In the wake of a growing, locally organized protest virtually everywhere, African colonies achieved their independence in three ways: by negotiation, by defiance, and by military struggle.

In the large number of cases where independence was negotiated, it marked not a rupture but a redefinition, guaranteeing by the design of Paris or London or Brussels a status of senior partner to the metropole and its interests. In most cases, colonial powers had orchestrated and manipulated the process of decolonization to exclude the most uncompromising, the most intransigent, and the most stubborn aspirant leaders in the colonies.

As a result of this controlled process of decolonization, the newly emerging African leaders were usually too preoccupied to see beyond the immediate struggle or failed to understand the reality of political independence as a means to an end, rather than as the end in itself. They moved into accommodations and offices vacated by white administrators, and, before full independence, accepted that everything should be done as the colonizer wanted it done, to secure his seal of approval.

Nor did those from the metropole occupying senior positions in the years leading to independence throw themselves wholeheartedly into preparing Africans to function efficiently in an essentially foreign administrative context, the top of which they had scarcely been allowed even to glimpse. An African leader tells the story of how, on becoming chief minister before his country's full independence, the only available model for his first minute to the colonial governor was a note, starting with Y.E., and written for his guidance by the expatriate permanent secretary. Not wishing to exhibit ignorance, the chief minister continued to open all minutes, including those to his subordinates, with those two initials. Only after some time did the permanent secretary let him know that Y.E. stood, of course, for "Your Excellency."

Most of the props of colonial subjugation were left in place. Where changes were brought about, they had to be such that they did not adversely affect the senior-partner standing of the metropole or its interests. An African leader threatening this relationship would feel great pressure to make him fall back into line. Another reaction was possible though—to move to the other extreme, seeking friendship and association with the Socialist bloc, by definition opposed to the Western bloc that included all European colonizing powers.

Only Guinea achieved political independence by defiance, paying dearly at the hands of France for doing so. Not only did the virtual overnight disruption of its political structure follow, but so did sabotage of everything from government files to telephones. It may not be overstating the case to say that leaders in Francophone Africa have never completely forgotten the lesson.

Guinea's reaction was not in the first instance, however, to turn against the West and it asked the United States in particular for help. Refusal brought a predictable reaction: bitterness followed by a turn to the East. (Sékou Touré could hardly have been expected to be sympathetic to concerns that put NATO allegiances ahead of oft-repeated principles.)

Thus with decolonization most former colonies remained substantially within the areas of influence of the former colonial powers. For countries that had to fight for their independence, however, the situation was different. Having taken up arms against their colonizers, they could not, once free, easily fraternize with those they had been fighting.

Since the Western bloc's code of conduct does not admit of overt military support for freedom fighters seeking independence from another of the bloc's members, the main source of military hardware and support for such freedom fighters is normally the Socialist bloc, although the more liberal Scandinavian and Third World countries also contribute. Leaders of such newly liberated nations tended to seek association and identification with a socialist ideological alternative. It should not have surprised anyone that they were likely to do so, both to show gratitude and to move away from capitalism, for socialism was seen more and more as decades of polarization pass as the only alternative to capitalism, the twin brother of colonial and racial oppression. This ideological dichotomizing has opened the way for heightened East-West rivalry in Africa, making the task of consolidation and cooperation within Africa more difficult.

But in all cases, the new leaders of Africa have had to assume political and other responsibilities for which they were ill-equipped. Most of them have had to "battle" on nonetheless and, however badly prepared, confront, essentially unaided, the awesome problems of development and nation-building.

Along with the colonial structures and machinery of government and politics, most of the emergent African countries inherited or rapidly acquired the consumption patterns and tastes of industrialized and developed economies without the attendant production techniques and skills. They seemed to believe in development based on consumption rather than production. Large civil service bureaucracies and parastatals were built to provide unproductive jobs and to pay political debts, without taking into account the resource base that was necessary to support so unwieldy a state apparatus. In time, the seemingly reckless pursuit of programs of state expansion progressively undermined the equilibrium between consumption and the resource base.

In some cases, the life style of the new rulership even helped to undermine that resource base. In some parts of my own country, Nigeria, the new government, having come into power with the slogan "Life More Abundant," was determined to provide a concrete example of what that meant. They swapped their small-size British-built cars for large and more imposing American models. They caught a veritable spending fever. With the leaders in such a "life more abundant" mood, their followers could hardly be in a hardworking mood. They could only be in a "high life" and quick money-making mood. (We even have music called "High Life.")

In post-World War II Africa—in the British colonies at least—the educated Africans could be broadly divided into three groups. The brightest at school immediately joined the colonial civil service or went to work for European trading companies, mainly as clerks. From there, some of them were able to train as professionals, and many remained in the civil service. By law, civil servants were not allowed to participate in politics, although in some cases they were pressured into resigning and entering the political fray.

The second group, what I call the second-best at school, managed to further their education by their own efforts, usually in metropolitan countries, and eventually became self-employed or underemployed. The law did not prevent them from taking part in politics, and they made up the largest group, into whose ready hands politics fell.

The third group comprised the school drop-outs, either underemployed or unemployed, who became errand boys for the politicians. Overnight they became contractors, acting as fronts for the politicians, conduits through whom money was siphoned to finance political parties. In the process money also found its way into private pockets, making some of the school drop-outs wealthy, while the second group, with political power and authority, also had substantial financial resources.

Those of the first group, the brightest and the best, who remained as civil servants and private sector employees, technically and generally had no political and economic power, nor as much influence as their other two brothers. Yet with their known background, they were expected in their villages and communities to play the role of local leaders, which might well cost more money than they could legitimately earn. The corruption which started with politicians seeking money to finance their campaigns and political parties soon pervaded the whole fabric of society, including the military.

Let me relate the persistence of this problem to my country, Nigeria. Even with the thirteen years of military administration from 1966 to 1979, and especially the last four of those years in which we dealt severely with corruption and inefficiency by dismissing over 10,000 public servants and recovering ill-gotten gains of political office holders and civil servants, the disease merely remained dormant. At the earliest opportunity, with the resumption of political activities, it spread with greater virulence than ever before.

Nor did the provision of public funds to finance reasonable political party activities during election campaigns dispel corruption in politics, once the military had supervised the first election and left the scene. It turned out that most of the political parties had borrowed heavily to supplement the public funding provided during the first election, and literally went on a rampage on assuming office.

What made things worse this time around in Nigeria was the availability of oil money and the involvement of foreign businessmen who, in collaboration with Nigerians, embarked on over-invoicing and payment without supplying goods at all, or, scarcely better, providing grossly inferior services and goods. Corruption became more pervasive, the amounts involved more colossal, and—compounding the damage to the nation—the money was siphoned out of the country with the assistance of foreign accomplices. The inspection of goods to be imported, a measure I introduced to counter these abuses, only marginally reduced them, once the political days returned; the inspectors were simply subverted. It turned out that other measures—such as dismissal from the public service, prohibition of holding office in future, and the recovery of discovered ill-gotten gains—also proved inadequate. It seemed that those against whom corruption and abuse of office could be proved would have to be sentenced to stiff terms of imprisonment as well.

But whatever actions we may take to stem the tide of corruption, we must have the assistance of our trading partners—especially from the West and Third World countries—in order to succeed. The banks, particularly, will have to be persuaded to be more open and more willing to seek out and expose deposits of a dubious nature, and to repatriate such accounts to the countries of origin. The concerted international efforts needed here will require national legislation and action similar in scope and necessary attention to the current collaborative efforts against the drug traffic.

Indeed, I would propose linking the two international problems in the search for solutions. Capital flight through corruption is damaging to the country of origin and beneficial to the recipient country. Drug trafficking brings social, economic, and security damage to the recipient country, while benefiting financially the country of origin. Such linkage ought to galvanize support from both ends to deal with these two menacing problems, for drugs are sapping the strength of the industrialized world and capital flight through corruption is similarly wounding the Third World. I would in fact go further to suggest making official development assistance contingent on a country's taking effective steps to curb corruption and adhering to any international agreements on that subject. To prevent the diversion of loans made by private banks, it may be necessary, as a first step, to establish joint commissions comprising representatives from the banks and recipient governments to monitor the use of the money. This could well be seen as infringing on national sovereignty. But it is vastly preferable to the consequences of a sudden and dramatic reduction in credit flows imposed unilaterally by banks.

The cultural disorientation that has given rise to such distorted behavior in African political processes is not the only significant legacy of colonial rule. Another in the British system is the practice of having an institutionalized opposition, a concept not only alien but profoundly incongruent with most African political culture and practice, in which government functioned by consensus. In many African languages the word "opposition" is the same as that for "enemy." How can one conceptualize a loyal enemy?

Further, since an enemy is supposed to be ruthlessly dealt with or even destroyed, most of Africa's inheritors of political independence spent inordinate time not only "establishing" themselves to ensure personal and political survival, but also hunting down and dealing with "enemies," real and imagined. The kind-hearted allowed their opposition to go into exile or put them in prison; others put theirs under the soil. Human rights questions apart, these actions prompted by fear diverted leaders from the more imperative task of nation-building and gravely exacerbated divisions within society.

Nor were these problems of political turmoil the only

ones new African countries had to face. Before long, economic stagnation, or even retrogression, and social disintegration and unrest would follow. The initial mood of optimism, hope, and high expectations was overtaken by frustration and pessimism. With distrust and disillusionment setting in, the military stepped in, in many countries, to hold together the fragile fabric of the state. In doing so initially, they reawakened the expectations that had greeted the continent from within and without at the time of independence.

The ordinary people of Africa had expected that with their own kith and kin running affairs, their lives would change for the better. Most of the leaders had a genuine desire to perform, but they lacked vision, and they lacked experience. Some well-disposed foreigners had also thought that, with political responsibilities in African hands, the continent they saw as a sleeping giant would be full of energy and progress. But African leaders, civilian and military alike, have only partially been able to fulfill these expectations, whatever their source. Here, sadly, lies the convergence of myth and reality in today's Africa.

The pace of change in the late twentieth century has forced upon Africa problems that no one had imagined three decades ago. Similarly, we will have to think carefully about finding solutions that are outside conventional answers and may go beyond ideological constraints.

To my mind, the greatest instrument of change that is substantially out of the control of African leaders (be they politicians, soldiers, businessmen, administrators, or farmers) is the instant communication, with its biases and its destructive power, being beamed into and out of Africa. Within any African country, any disparaging statement by a member of one ethnic group against members of another can be exaggerated and manipulated to become a serious political issue.

In settled societies such as Britain, or a melting pot like the United States, one group of citizens may make statements against another group that may go unnoticed, though even here media reports of such slurs do often provoke outcries and more. But in young and weak African nations, with their fragile fabrics of integration and cohesion, the irresponsible use of the instruments of mass communication may destroy such countries irreparably, rather than serve to establish a culture of democracy. It is vital that the mass media be used with caution, maturity, understanding, restraint, and responsibility.

A number of African countries are now seeking, by painful processes of trial and error, new political structures and systems, rooted in their traditional culture and truly representative, with democratic principles of human rights and obligations, freedom with responsibility, and peaceful and orderly succession. If such systems and structures are to evolve, like those of most settled industrial societies, it will take time.

But whatever they are, they must be our own, designed by ourselves, for ourselves. They may not at all points meet the democratic ideals, principles, and practices as designed in the West, but we must be free to learn from our own past and from history. In politics and governance, as indeed in all walks of life, Africa must not be judged according to the cultural values of the West.

Let me turn to my own country's experience. In Nigeria, we tried both parliamentary and presidential forms of government, with up to five parties, unsuccessfully. To me, the fault has lain less in the systems than in their operators. Indeed, except on such matters as the number and duration of terms for a president, I see not much wrong in the Constitution and attendant political arrangements my administration bequeathed to Nigeria.

As a military administration, we did not arrogate to ourselves the production entirely on our own of a new Constitution for the country. Rather, we set up a Constitutional Drafting Committee, consisting of forty-nine men (one having opted out). They submitted their draft constitution a year later, and it was translated into the three main languages of the country, published, and debated for another year. Then came a largely elected Constituent Assembly (10 percent of its members were nominated to represent such underrepresented interests as women and students). This body worked for almost a year to present the Constitution that, with a few minor changes, was approved by the military administration and became law.

Our Constitution has been described as being modeled on that of the United States. To the extent that we opted for an executive presidency and the separation of powers, it did indeed derive inspiration from that remarkable document, about to celebrate its 200th anniversary. But in essential respects ours was Nigerian, taking cognizance of peculiarly Nigerian factors.

We chose to have an executive presidency because our first constitution, modeled on the British parliamentary system, had led to confusion and conflict between the authority of the president, who in some sense reigned, and the prime minister who ruled. Further, Nigerian culture by and large admits of only one chief or king to reign and rule.

The multinational character of our society, meanwhile, has made a federal form of government imperative. Ours has come to have nineteen states, so that no single one can hold the whole nation in ransom through its size, resources, or strategic importance. And to ensure that no "tribal baron" can become leader of the nation with only tribal support, our 1979 Constitution required a president not only to have the largest number of votes cast, but also to show significant support (25 percent of votes cast) in at least two-thirds of the states. Further, the president has to have a cabinet minister from each of the nineteen states, whether or not he received significant support in all.

Revenue allocation, to be fair, has been made to take both population and the sources of revenue into account, among other factors, with all three tiers of government—central, state, and local—included in the formula. But for all of those measures, we have not yet solved the essential problem of how to bring forth national leaders without violence, recriminations, and bitterness. More about that later.

I believe there are certain requirements for any successful political system in Africa. First, it must involve the people, all the people. Involvement may come through discussion and debate, selection or election. Governments have thus far tended to secure votes from the people once every few years and ignore them between elections.

Second, the government must be truly representative in terms of geography and population, so that no major interests go unrepresented.

Third, human rights and respect for human dignity, with citizens' obligations and duties spelled out, must be enshrined. The gross abuse and violations we have witnessed at the hands of both military and civilian regimes in Africa must not recur if we are to respect ourselves within the comity of nations. But our citizens must also be made to understand that there are sacred obligations, duties, and responsibilities which they owe to the corporate existence of their countries, in the interest of the welfare of all and of their individual well-being. Peaceful and orderly successions are essential, and evolving mechanisms to ensure them must be among Africa's highest priorities.

Fourth, freedom of expression without endangering the corporate existence of the nation must be preserved. The objectives of the government must be clear, unambiguous and, not least, followed. There must be rules of the political game agreed upon, and the players must observe them.

This brings us to a set of components generally believed essential to the functioning of a democracy: political parties. In 1979, I refrained for three reasons from decreeing a one- or two-party system for Nigeria. First, it would have amounted to a major amendment to the constitutional draft as presented by the Constituent Assembly, and I had already decided against making substantial changes. Second, a two-party system would likely have ended in a geographical division, exacerbating one of our most persistent tensions, the north-south dichotomy, and thereby increasing instability. Third, I believed then and do now that such determinations should come through evolution, not legislation.

In fact, we were beginning on such an evolutionary course when, out of some fifty-two applications, only five parties satisfied the conditions for registration in 1979; after the 1983 elections, only four parties remained in essence. If we had had two more elections without interruption, I could have seen one or, at most, two parties remaining active.

I do not believe it appropriate to advocate one political arrangement or system of government for all countries of Africa. In a few countries where there has been some enduring political and governmental continuity, it has grown out of charismatic leadership taking a pragmatic, rather than a doctrinaire, approach to political, social and economic management. Indeed, it seems to me that in some cases a one-party system with such characteristics can move a country along a path of harmony and political stability within a durable structure. I say this, knowing the disinclination of supporters of Western-style democracy—which I too admire and have tried—to see any virtue in having fewer than two parties. An institutionalized loyal opposition may be a luxury Africa cannot afford right now.

With sixty-nine successful coups d'état in Africa since independence, and fifteen current military governments in place (not counting those that have metamorphosed through a change from uniforms into civilian dress), the military must be seen as a reality on Africa's political scene well into the twenty-first century.

While the records of few governments (past and present, military and non-military) in Africa can be described as monstrous, and while none of the current military governments in Africa will pass the litmus test of democracy *à la West*, not all military regimes are unrepresentative and more tyrannical, corrupt, or servile to external interests than the civilian governments they replaced. Although our population is comparatively high, our utilizable skilled, experienced, and trained manpower is severely limited. We need the services of all, military and civilian alike. Further, in a situation of inherent or recurrent instability, military government may be inevitable, no matter what one might wish in principle.

Even in the best of times, under stable civilian rule and political order, it may well be both necessary and rational to associate or harness the military in the process of nation-building and development. Whereas there may be advantages in the singleness of purpose of a good military administration in formulating and executing development programs, I do also see substantial advantages in the cohesive and integrative force generated through healthy political activities that are not part of military rule.

Some people have seriously talked of diarchy, which in the African context has come to mean a form of government in which civilians and the military participate on an equal footing. In the true British tradition, I believe that the military must contribute to the process of nation-building, particularly in the context of defending the integrity of the nation. If for any reason the military have to intervene in the political system, they must be able to take full responsibility for their action.

Whoever leads in Africa, civilian or military, has to face imperatives that call for a particular type of comprehension of his responsibilities, duties, and obligations. Such leaders will require a special type of preparation and exposure to carry them out. Most of them have been focusing their attention primarily on single issues and have had no time to look at the wider and critical regional and global questions that are all impinging on Africa's future. For potential African leaders, time for comprehensive study, reflection, and sharing experiences with persons within and outside their country, region, and specific field is very limited, and the opportunities for doing so are rare.

Once top leadership and executive positions come, those holding them have little opportunity to acquire the skills and perspectives they need. Yet they must have clear regional and global perspectives, sensitivity to and understanding of national development needs, and the ability to work with other leaders to solve pressing problems. There are virtually no institutions in Africa devoted to preparing leaders so that they can cooperate within and across national, regional, and institutional boundaries.

Relatedly, in most African countries it is difficult, if not impossible, to gain access to relevant and timely information on key national, regional, and global issues. African leaders and non-Africans interested in the continent's future and the implications of that future for the world must act to correct this serious situation. Emerging and promising African leaders must have a forum providing exposure and interaction to enable them to seek solutions to joint problems together with other leaders. The issues of development, peace and security, sustaining the world economy, and improving the environment are universal, interrelated, and global and cannot be solved by uncoordinated action, in Africa or elsewhere.

There is no point in romanticizing a past that, even if it had been perfect, will not come back to us. But there are aspects of our culture and previous political traditions that we can modernize and graft onto new realities and new situations. Perhaps we should reconsider political campaigns and elections to choose our leaders, given the heavy costs, the corruption, the accompanying bitterness, recriminations, and dissatisfaction. Perhaps we should instead enlist the age-old practice of sounding out local opinion, and selecting representatives within communities, with urban centers being divided into wards and quarters. Nor should this process seem totally foreign to anyone familiar with the way in which British political parties choose their candidates for "safe" seats.

In any case, from this essentially traditional African democratic procedure, I would then secure representation to legislative bodies at the state and national level by a series of indirect elections. Whether the chief executive would emerge from the national legislature or be chosen by a separate process, or by some imaginative combination of both, would depend on the special circumstances of a given country. I would hope that this process could reduce the deleterious emphasis on the politics of resource distribution and ethnicity; it could be an African way to infuse a modern political system with a new sense of values, placing a premium on qualities of leadership and character.

But we need not only, at one end of the scale of size, to recapture the sense of genuine representation from and at the local level, we need also to reconsider at the other end the number of nation-states on the African continent. If Europeans, our erstwhile colonizers, are coming together politically, economically, scientifically, and in the area of defense and security in order to coordinate effective action and have a voice in the world, ought not we in Africa to question maintaining divisions arbitrarily created for us by outsiders in the nineteenth century? We have fifty-four countries in Africa; we have too many countries.

These divisions into a plethora of mostly small states sap our political strength. However attractive the thought of receiving top protocol treatment, African leaders must realize that a century ago, when outsiders drew these boundaries, nations were far less interdependent than they are now. The very arbitrariness of these boundaries should encourage us to think again, and deeply, about them, as many observers expected us to do at the time of independence in protest against their colonial artificiality.

Today, in our ever-shrinking world, it is vitally important to cooperate and, eventually, coalesce in order to have adequate control over the changes that are bombarding all of us. Many nations, including the superpowers, have found that they have to work with others in such areas as security, the economy, trade, the environment, and health. For Africa such cooperation must be the new imperative.

The Organization of African Unity (OAU) must actively encourage countries that have any inclination to come together economically and politically to form larger and more viable units. More difficult, countries themselves must come to recognize that it is in their interest to surrender some aspects of sovereignty; that, indeed, in a stronger polity, possibly confederal in form, their sovereignty would be enhanced. Greater population, land area, economic and military strength, if resting on a base of stable and durable political institutions, would give them not only greater security but also greater genuine independence.

In 1975 the West African sub-region started an experiment with potential along these lines, the Economic Community of West African States (ECOWAS). In 1976 ECOWAS was explicitly acknowledged as a forerunner of a confederation of West African states with its impressive land area, resources, market, and growth potential. The phases of development would be substantially along the lines of the European Economic Community, starting with economic cooperation, defense and security agreements, and nonaggression pacts, and moving on to economic integration, the gradual surrender of sovereignty for the common good and political cooperation, reaching finally common citizenship and a common parliament.

Economic collaboration and common defense and security are easier issues to tackle, in Africa as in Europe, than is political consolidation. As in Europe, Africans have to deal with problems of language that divide them; but ironically, in West Africa especially, the languages of political divisions are European, mirroring colonial education and administration. African leadership with vision can use that very fact to surmount the difficulty by appealing to pre-colonial historical pride. But it will have to be done with skill, for African historical rivalries and fears of domination need allaying as much as do those encouraged by the colonial era's definitions of nation.

ECOWAS surmounted the initial problems facing it from within the region and from those outside who wished to maintain long-established economic spheres of influence. After 1979, however, the momentum waned, and from 1982 on—when the impact of world recession and mounting debt began to take their toll on the more promising West African economies—the tensions that come with economic contraction made neighbors turn on each other as unrest and hardship mounted within their borders. Africans expelled "foreign" workers, just as Europeans have done, setting back the cause of regional cooperation.

I see no viable future for many African states, and perhaps for all of them politically, however, unless such organizations as ECOWAS become a living and active reality, leading to economic, security, and political cooperation, consolidation, and integration within Africa's principal regions. I should like to see African leaders work concertedly toward creating six confederations in the twenty-first century.

I believe that the larger the political entities that make up Africa, the greater will be their stability in the long run. We must realize the advantages in size and in the economies of scale. I do not minimize the difficulties of persuading many Africans to see these larger issues. Most of the largest African countries—Zaire, Nigeria, the Sudan, and Ethiopia, for example—have faced the threat or reality of civil war. Yet none of them has broken up, and it is my judgment that none is likely to do so. Unquestionably, however, the weaker Africa's economic circumstances, the less likely we are to see broader vision prevail; we all know that conditions of scarcity and insecurity rarely bring out generous instincts.

The Western world has, until now, tended to concern itself little with the political or economic health of Africa, perpetuating instead a superficial view based in part on the myths we have discussed, in part because of perceived self-interest in thus maintaining their own economic and political dominance. We are entering an era, however, in which even the United States is having to recognize global economic interdependence in ways unimaginable only a few years ago. It may not be too long before the need to strengthen African economies may be viewed as essential to healthy First World economies, a subject I shall take up in the next chapter. But such measures can only assist African leaders as they struggle to find the way to political stability for the continent—surely a development of importance to the entire world.

Africans meanwhile will need to dispense with myths they hold dear, not least because in doing so they will start a process that will in itself dispel the surviving myths about them in the Western world. It is the Africans who need urgently to shed their blinders about the essential challenges of economic, social, and political development. They must come to accept that an unjust international order will not change simply because of the euphony of their own rhetoric or the indignation accompanying their moral pressure.

They must seriously organize and mobilize their societies for a more profound and sustained development process, predicated on the conviction that they cannot have development without sacrifice. They must inculcate in all their citizens the conviction that development means hard work, sweat, forbearance, and discipline. They must reach down into the base of their cultural fountain and bring up new sustenance from age-old values, norms, and ideals so that they can address the challenges posed by a largely unsympathetic world leaving them behind.

The Balkanization of Africa has weakened the continent both internally and in relation to the rest of the world. Many have come to believe that African views on critical global issues, both economic and political, carry no weight because no effective action is seen to stand behind them, not even when the pressing issues are on their own continent. Africans themselves must take the lead in making themselves matter in the world in which they live. They can only be helped by friends and well-wishers, acting out of common citizenship of the earth, our common heritage.

TWO

Debt, Disarmament, and Development

In the last chapter, I examined mainly the political situation in Africa north of the Limpopo, suggesting at the same time that its challenges cannot be met without understanding and changing the economic environment of the continent. Those seeking to address or redress Africa's economic ills generally focus on policies within specific countries or, at most, regions of the continent itself, and I shall turn to those presently. But it must be clear at the outset that Africa, possibly even more than other regions of our interdependent world, cannot have its economic problems adequately assessed without paying more than passing attention to the world economy within which African countries must function.

Particularly since the early 1980s, reactivation of a stagnating world economy has moved by fits and starts. Debt crises in most countries of Latin America and Africa and some socialist countries have combined with deficit budgeting in market economy countries, most notably the United States, to produce far-reaching consequences. The handling of Third World debt has at least stalled development, in some cases actually reversing it, in the debtor countries, while creating unemployment in most industrialized countries of the Organization for Economic Cooperation and Development (OECD).

Most Latin American and African debtors have drastically cut imports and subsidized exports in order to service their debts, making it difficult for European and American industrial and farm products to enter these markets. Short-term bridge loans arranged by the International Monetary Fund (IMF), the London Club, or the Paris Club have not rekindled economic growth and development; instead they have only served—as intended—to finance debt service and repayment.

Indeed, rationalization of their economies by most Third World debtor nations has halted internal investment and exacerbated capital flight. Structural adjustment programs, which of necessity require austerity and curtailing expenditure, have in most countries not produced transformed productive structures, stabilization, and increased capital formation. Rather, the conditionalities required by the international financial community are stringent, creditor-protecting, and destabilizing to the debtor countries, often creating conditions profoundly threatening to their economic, social, and political fabrics.

The debt problem was not created by the actions of the debtor nations alone. They were goaded by commercial banks, which had surplus deposits of petrodollars to recycle, and the creditor nations, which supported their banks. Let me digress for a moment here to share with you my own experience. In 1977 and 1978, at the time of a slight dip in the oil market, international bankers were descending upon my government in droves. They pressed the case that our economic strength was such that we were grossly underborrowed, especially for a nation with such a visionary development program. All that led to our first jumbo loan of what seems now a mere $1 billion. Unfortunately, our successors in government succumbed more readily to the bankers' siren song, which led to our current debt of some $20 billion, assuring us membership in the distinguished club of insolvent Third World countries.

Thus commercial banks as well as debtor and creditor nations have joint responsibility to seek solutions to the debt problems. Thus far cooperation among central banks and the skillful responses of the IMF, the World Bank, and the Bank for International Settlements have succeeded in containing the crisis. But sadly I must stress that thus far they have merely contained the problem, not solved it. Despite these efforts, no debtor country has seen a decline in its overall debt since the crisis began in 1982. Even worse, the Third World debtors have all become net capital exporters to the developed world, to such an extent that they can no longer meet their primary responsibilities to their populations. This situation, if unchecked, is bound to threaten the stability and independence as well as the democratic aspirations of these nations.

It is politically intolerable that as a result of fluctuations in interest and exchange rates the debtor countries cannot predict the maximum debt-service payments they must make, in dollars, during the year ahead. This uncertainty continues to have a devastating effect on national planning and development.

Thus the commercial banks and creditor nations should take into account the vital needs of debtor countries in bringing about a lowering of world interest rates and trade expansion. The situation has deteriorated to such a degree that creditor nations must adopt urgent measures to enable commercial banks to grant moratoriums as immediate relief without jeopardizing the flow of fresh money. They should also provide comparable fresh financial resources and relief through institutions such as the Paris Club. International financial institutions must receive financial resources commensurate to their tasks. The IMF and the World Bank must devise a lasting solution to the debt problem, one that will involve the commercial banks, the creditor countries, the debtor countries, and the international financial and development organizations in joint burden-sharing.

The contribution of commercial banks should not be limited to protecting themselves against possible bad debts, but should include providing relief and fresh money in instances where a debtor country shows a good-faith commitment to adhere to an agreed-upon adjustment program. The United States must take legislative measures to protect and strengthen American commercial banks against possible sudden default, collapse, or near-bankruptcy of a debtor nation in the manner that European countries do through reserve requirement provisions. Major lending countries need to harmonize these arrangements.

To contain annual debt repayments where they become excessive and destabilizing, necessary steps should include:

a) restriction of annual debt-service payments to an agreed maximum that will allow for continuous investment, growth, and development;
b) consolidation of short-term debts into medium- and long-term fixed-interest bonds;
c) capitalization of interest;
d) forgiveness on OECD Official Development Assistance loans to least developed countries in the first instance, and to other developing countries on a case-by-case basis;
e) debt and interest-rate relief on a country-by-country, case-by-case basis.

I do not advocate unilateral repudiation of debt, even in the dire circumstances most African debtor nations face. But there can be no ignoring their temptation to insist on unilateral action, or at least on suspending payment, as Ecuador has just done in the face of its catastrophic earthquake, following on Brazil's unilateral suspension of interest payment for three months. Debt-servicing must be kept to an amount that allows for reasonable growth and development. It is in everyone's best interest to have such a level negotiated and agreed upon; otherwise, to avoid self-destruction, debtor nations may have to fix the level themselves.

The plan announced by Secretary of the Treasury James A. Baker in Seoul, South Korea, in September 1985 addressed some of these issues. The Baker Plan asked commercial banks to provide $20 billion and multilateral agents $9 billion over a three-year period; any badly debt-ridden country implementing the conditionalities of tax cuts, budget cuts, minimum wage cuts, and large-scale privatization would be eligible for loans against these funds.

The emphasis was to be on growth; but since the Baker Plan does not allow for interest-rate and debt relief, it merely increases debt, exposing banks to a greater possibility of default. Worse, the mounting debt simply stimulates greater capital flight and prolongs the very policies that created the debt crisis.

Even though the Baker Plan did not, therefore, provide an adequate solution to the debt crisis, it was refreshingly welcome. For the first time an OECD country—indeed, the leader of the industrialized countries—admitted, even if only by implication, that the debt problem was jointly created and must be jointly addressed. But it is just a beginning. Capital flight that results from corruption and mismanagement of Third World economies will not stop with granting more loans. Taking measures to inhibit drastically such acts in any debtor country must be part of the debt and interest-rate relief essential if Third World debtors are to help themselves restore investment, growth, and development.

Debt relief has to be a central concern. Debt relief should not be defined as weakening creditworthiness. Furthermore, it should be provided on a country-by-country basis, with no case becoming a precedent, and with the special aim of financing debtor efforts to improve growth and investor confidence. Such relief, offered on a multilateral basis to insure uniform standards, should not adversely affect the rest of the loan portfolios of banks. The alternative that an increasing debt burden can cause—namely unilateral debt repudiation— could lead to a serious banking crisis and would certainly damage the defaulter's creditworthiness. Such developments are desirable for no one.

Resolving the debt crisis will remain a mirage for as long as the largest national economy in the world also induces the largest net capital inflow from other economies as a result of persistent and high budget deficits. Action to reduce the U.S. budget deficit is imperative for sustainable revitalization of the world economy. This is far from simply an American domestic issue; it is one with dire implications for us elsewhere in the world, particularly in Africa.

Expenditure on arms is central both to the issue of the American budget deficit and, more broadly, to questions of revitalizing the world economy and of development in Third World countries. Lack of progress in arms-reduction negotiations, the continuing escalation in research into ever more far-reaching systems, and stockpiling what is now available all combine to increase the danger of nuclear confrontation with all its unimaginable annihilating consequences. The unabated arms race between the superpowers and their allies combine with conflicts among developing countries to drain resources urgently needed for development. The continuing gulf between the superpowers and their unremitting preparatory efforts for possible war on the one hand and, on the other, the debilitating debt burden of most developing countries and the conflicts among them tend to widen the gap between developing and developed countries. The misapplication of resources by East, West, North, or South compounds the difficulty of revitalizing the world economy.

At the same time pressures for protectionism are mounting—against products from Third World and other OECD countries alike—a particularly discouraging development in view of the central role trade policies play in restoring sustained global economic growth and resolving the debt crisis. Over 50 percent of world trade is now restricted by protectionist measures or distorted by subsidies. Indeed, over $120 billion is paid in a single year as subsidies of agricultural products in the nations of the North.

While some measure of protection may be understandable for pioneer industries in developing countries, the broader trend toward protectionism with its attendant deterioration in trade relations must be arrested and, indeed, reversed. Determined efforts must restore the effectiveness of the General Agreement on Tariffs and Trade (GATT), bringing governments back under the multilateral discipline of mutual rights and obligations it embodies.

Further, the new round of trade negotiations must result in arresting the spread of narrow economic nationalism, especially among major trading nations; such a new round must contribute to restoring confidence in the multilateral approach to managing trade relations. A commitment by the major trading nations to submit their restrictive actions, both formal and informal, to multilateral scrutiny within the GATT framework would go a long way toward arresting the spread of protectionism which, unchecked, will surely lead to world economic stagnation and strangulation. Developed countries should reduce tariff and non-tariff trade restrictions, particularly on exports from developing countries, while also encouraging economic cooperation among them, making way for expanding trade in both directions.

International cooperation is invariably frustrated by institutional rigidities. While all acknowledge the intimate connection between the world's trade and financial problems, no one seems able to break through the now traditional compartmentalization to deal with the totality of the world economic crisis. Support for new projects in agriculture and industry and to provide socio-economic infrastructure will be futile in an atmosphere of trade restriction, protectionism, low commodity prices, and without regard to capital flow. The present volatile monetary arrangements have proved generally unhelpful to expanding international trade. A new consensus among especially the major economic powers over international monetary reform is essential.

Let me return to disarmament and military expenditures to take up more fully their implications for developing countries in general and Africa in particular. The failure of the superpowers to reduce their arsenals of nuclear weapons has provided a bad example for other states. As vertical proliferation continues, horizontal proliferation remains at best only marginally restrained. Nations, to maintain regional superiority over their identified adversaries, aspire to be able to produce nuclear weapons with the assistance and support of industrialized, nuclear-capable countries.

If the already heavily armed superpowers and their allies rationalize ever-increasing armaments in the name of security, rather than seek common security with their identified adversaries, how can one persuade weak and struggling nations of any other way to assure their own security? It is unlikely that many countries, or any region for that matter, would wish to disarm in conditions of intense global armament and insecurity fanned by unbridled arms competition. The effect of the global disarmament effort on regional disarmament is direct, for disarmament in any one region can hardly proceed independent of what obtains in the rest of the world.

African attitudes toward disarmament must be seen in this context. The nuclear arms race and the prospect of nuclear disaster pose a major threat to Africa in particular. Any deterioration in the relationship between the superpowers which aggravates global instability and increases the capacity of either country to play a disruptive role in regional conflicts must have its impact there. As we have seen, the regional and security concerns of Africa focus on preserving existing territorial delimitations and on nation-building while containing disintegrative tendencies.

Because of these concerns and regional conflicts that have grown out of them, most African countries are diverted at one time or another from the essential task of concentrating on their development. Leaders tend to spend far too much time on personal and political survival, draining the energy they should be giving to key social and economic issues. They must instead concentrate on adopting fair, equitable, and socially just policies to enhance harmony within their countries. To do so will in fact reduce the threat to their survival. They must also strengthen bilateral and sub-regional economic cooperation, out of which formal security arrangements can grow to promote self-restraint in military expenditures and the acquisition of certain types of weapons.

Africa faces more than enough complicating natural disasters—among them drought, desertification, insects, disease, and escalating and uncontrolled population growth—without further compounding its international problems of debt and deteriorating terms of trade through arms races and East-West confrontations.

The greatest handicap of African leaders in formulating development policy at the time of independence was their lack of adequate experience and exposure in economic matters. Economic advisers, black and white, prescribed solutions that turned out to be at best half-successful, being often poorly conceived and ill-adapted to Africa's needs. The most glaring single example of failure was the widely touted policy of import substitution, which, as designed for us, made us into assemblers of finished and semi-finished goods from the west, rather than manufacturers in our own right. Even our own agricultural products were sent first to the industrialized countries to be processed and were only returned to us to be packaged.

Before independence, most African people had been brought up to rely almost absolutely on their environment, their maker, and their own efforts. Post-independence economic development programs, however, largely ignored the rural areas, where most of the people were living, failing to stress skills bringing greater self-reliance. We tended to seek easy solutions in our agricultural, industrial, and educational development.

We opted for projects rather than programs, and the grander the projects, the more appealing they were to politicians, military men, and bureaucrats alike. We seemed good at diagnosis and rhetoric, but poor in action and performance. In order to satisfy those swelling the populations of the cities, where they could shout and organize to cause political and social unrest to plague governments, we poured more and more of our meager available resources into urban centers, neglecting rural areas the more and compounding the flow of people into the cities. The result has been the now well-known neglect of agriculture, followed by the need to import substantial amounts of food.

Even in a country like Nigeria, the sudden increase in resources available through oil did not seem to break the pattern. We need a reasonable gestation period and sustained effort for agricultural policies and programs to develop into flourishing projects. Such policies and programs as I devised during my administration were either stifled or killed by our successors in government.

Enchanted by such terms as import substitution, foreign capital, transfer of technology, and official development assistance, Africa did not fare much better in industrialization. Mesmerized by what we believed the world owed us after all that colonialism had extracted from us, we failed to understand that development would involve pain and sacrifice; we seemed to expect it to come through outsiders without our paying the cost in discipline, sacrifice, and denial. Neither did we think through new educational methods and goals appropriate to our circumstances. We used borrowed ideas, borrowed experience and funds, and we engaged borrowed hands.

In short, in our development strategies and programs, not much if anything is ours. It need not have been so, and it certainly need not be so now. Through study, training, and interaction with other peoples we can acquire adequate knowledge and skills to adapt strategies to our cultures, norms, and environment. But policies, priorities, and emphases in education must be the right ones. Basic science is essential, and the disciplines of stark survival must, I believe, take precedence over those that are more purely cerebral. However rigid it may sound, I am certain that the first generation of students in African universities should have studied agriculture (or better still, farming), engineering, and medicine, leaving it to their children to add architecture and astronomy, and to their children's children to take up philosophy and poetry. But Nigeria's premier university at Ibadan started in 1948 with history, classics, and philosophy as its disciplines, and did not add engineering until the mid-1970s, almost thirty years later.

Technology, which apparently drives the world of the late twentieth century, is the product of science. It is in fact applied science, and cannot be developed without a science base. The transfer of technology is an illusion, a catchy phrase conjuring up images of high-level scientific and technical expertise willingly and altruistically handed over in gift-wrapping from the owner in the developed world to us in Africa and the rest of the Third World.

But as the product of human resourcefulness, technology cannot be transferred by imports and turn-key projects. We will have to work through our own educational institutions, utilizing exchanges of personnel and data, developing our own resourcefulness, and adapting by ourselves the products of other people's efforts to fit them to the needs of our environment. It will be long and hard work, no doubt demanding sacrifice; but if we go about it through our own institutions, essentially by ourselves and for ourselves, we may just end up with development, programs, and projects that work for us and that we understand. It is important to emphasize that political leadership must organize and harness talent from the local business and intellectual communities to achieve this aim. This is my idea of appropriate technology.

I have no doubt that if we continue with prolonged uneven development and underdevelopment in Africa, cataclysmic dangers lie ahead. Escalating social disruption, political instability, and massive movements of human beings could lead to the partial or total obliteration of countries. International trade and business as we know it could deteriorate into counter trade, or barter, on a massive scale. Greater intrusion of superpower rivalry could trigger a "rescue package," resulting in repartition into shared spheres of influence. This cannot be an attractive world order for anyone seeking peace and stability—let alone justice.

To head off such catastrophe we must concentrate our efforts in virtually all African countries on agriculture as the bedrock for economic development. Africa is fortunate that, although it does have problems of land tenure, they are easily surmountable, compared to the difficulties of land redistribution in Latin America. The highest priority must be a major effort to encourage and assist the small farmers, in whose name much has been said and little done. The number of medium-size holders will continue to increase, and they too must receive assistance. Large-scale farming is important, but given the fragility of Africa's soils and other problems particular to the continent, adopting inappropriate technology for such undertakings can do massive damage. Further, it would not do to compound income maldistribution by displacing small farmers without providing them satisfactory alternative means of livelihood. In Africa, until we achieve self-sufficiency in food production, our debt problem will be well-nigh insoluble.

Nor should industrialization be ignored. It must, however, be based not, as before, on assembling imported parts, processing imported raw materials, or packaging finished products. Rather, it must aim to process agricultural products and manufacture simple farm machinery and implements, appropriate transportation and communications equipment, and materials for the building industry. We ourselves must also produce the wherewithal to repair and maintain equipment and essential facilities.

It is not an easy task to assess accurately what has worked

and what has not in the economic sector in Africa. But when we consider that most African countries have been independent less than three decades, some accomplishments stand out. Provision of education for Africans has greatly increased, quantitatively at least, in those years. If normal indicators of gross national and domestic product have lately shown stagnation or worse, there is no doubt that health services have improved, raising life expectancy by more than ten years—though admittedly that new level of 50 years is shamefully low. In most parts of the continent, communications and transportation have improved substantially, albeit in varying degrees.

But such flat statements conceal the very real difficulties African governments have faced in trying to implement such improvements. Let me take the case of telecommunications in Nigeria to illustrate some of the pernicious problems that exist. At the outset of my administration, Nigeria, with an estimated population of some 100 million, had a total of 50,000 telephone lines, or one for each 20,000 people, as against one for 50 people in the more industrialized developing countries and about one for 10 in developed countries. Good transportation and communications systems are of course indispensable for coordinating, running, and managing a modern government and economy. We also believed that these networks are essential instruments of integration and unity. We set out gradually to provide 750,000 telephone lines in a period of some five years.

We had selected the crossbar switching system to replace the British "step-by-step" type. The crossbar system had become more popular and widely used all over the world, and it was produced by many more companies. We could indeed manufacture the equipment under license in Nigeria, as Romania and Brazil had done. We believed that by this change we could get more competitive bidding and also save time in implementing our telecommunications programs.

From more than fifteen multinational companies that

submitted bids for the supply of switching equipment, four eventually emerged as winners: ITT, Siemens of West Germany, Nippon Electric through Marubeni of Japan, and L.M. Ericson of Sweden. Switching equipment is just one of the three major essential requirements for telecommunications. The other two are transmission, which in our case was based mainly on microwave, but with coaxial cable and aerostat or balloon as effective backup (the balloons never got off the ground); and third, receivers which consist of cable from exchange switches and receiving boxes in homes and offices.

But even for the switching, we needed the equipment itself, the building to house the equipment, and the stand-by generators to ensure continuous use of the equipment. Although switching equipment manufacturers or suppliers are not normally manufacturers of air conditioning equipment or generators, we could have given the whole switching package, including the buildings, to them as turn-key projects.

We decided initially, however, against the turn-key idea to reduce costs, which we believed we could do by getting the items separately and assembling them under a team of experts chosen for that purpose in the ministry of communications. We also wanted Nigerians to be involved to gain experience. To our chagrin, Nigerian architects and contractors performed, we would learn much later, far below our expectations. The workmanship in almost all cases was well below standard. Walls and floors were too weak to take the weight of equipment to be placed on them. When equipment began to arrive, there were no buildings to put it in. Suppliers had to hire special warehouses to prevent deterioration. Thus projects billed to be completed in two years went to four years and beyond. Meanwhile, consumers became restive, and criticisms mounted while costs escalated. Even when and where there are funds and viable programs, and the will to implement them, other factors slow down development in Africa.

In some cases in Africa there has been a genuine desire to try to redistribute wealth, using the textbook method of social welfarism and the attendant inefficient centralization and bureaucratization. In trying to share out the unbaked cake, there being no oven available, what seems to have been distributed is poverty; and even that has been inefficiently done. Development aid has not been as successful as anticipated. In any case, aid never involved all partners as equals in designing and implementing projects, nor in maintaining and evaluating them. The fault should not be placed entirely at the door of the donor, for some recipient countries have not developed skilled, experienced personnel who could make the contribution of coequals.

Yet for the necessary investment, growth, and development it must have, Africa needs to see itself as being relatively on its own. If, as Africans, our recent past has been lived for us and our present appears not to be in our hands, then we must take our future firmly into our hands. In no sphere is this more vital, to us and to the interdependent world, than in the economic one.

THREE

Southern Africa: Apartheid and Beyond

M y first chapter attempted to highlight the factors (not entirely of their own making) that have militated against the political performance of leaders in independent Africa. But as I said, I believe leaders deserve understanding, encouragement and opportunities to widen their horizons in ways I have suggested. The second major problem, that of economic transformation, took up the preceding chapter. Let me now turn to the third: the system of apartheid in South Africa and its direct effect throughout the Southern African sub-region, and its implications for the continent and the world, especially the Western world. In discussing the Southern African situation, I will draw on my experience as a member of the Commonwealth Group of Eminent Persons.

What struck me on my first visit to South Africa was the natural beauty of the country, its economic achievement, and its crying human tragedy. Such a beautiful and economically strong country in Africa must be preserved for all South Africans, all Africans, and all citizens of the world.

Apartheid has been described by the United Nations General Assembly as "a crime against humanity." From what we saw on the ground, that description is no exaggeration. It is not a system to be reformed; it is a system to be uprooted. It is a system maintained by pervasive violence that, of course, provokes counterviolence from its victims. In fact, it is a tribute to the tolerance, forbearance, and resilience characteristic of African culture that for fifty years violence never entered into the tactics of seeking political participation and justice in South Africa.

Since 1984, when the constitutional "reforms"—which merely made clearer than ever the exclusion of the African majority—began the latest cycle of violence, the government has assumed that they could end resistance by unleashing massive repression, as they did after Sharpeville in 1960 and Soweto in 1976. They have even gone one step farther, with the most pervasive press censorship in their history. But this time the anger of the blacks and their determination to attain justice will not give way to such measures, even if another 25,000, including infants, are sent into detention.

The ingenuity of this government in devising instruments of oppression knows virtually no limit. One of their latest is fomenting what they call "black-on-black violence." Exploiting divisions that exist within any community, they skillfully identify those they can arm, pay, and organize into "vigilantes," whom they then unleash in the townships against opponents of apartheid. On the authority of no less an organization than the Black Sash—whose members, significantly all white women, have worked for over three decades for black rights—we know that government agents have released from jail hardened criminals, with the express purpose of having them kill targeted opponents of apartheid in exchange for remission of their sentences.

In spite of these additional oppressive measures, the situation among the black population has these characteristics: the United Democratic Front (UDF) maintains its importance as a non-racial, community-based, national umbrella against apartheid. The ungovernability of some black townships persists. The black trade union movements continue their growth and political influence. The popularity and stature of Nelson Mandela as the black national leader increases despite his quarter-century of imprisonment. At the same time the African National Congress (ANC) has become the dominant black political force within the country, and mounts increased, if still sporadic, guerilla attacks.

In June 1986 the Eminent Persons Group submitted its report, in which we were forced by the South African government's rejection of our negotiating concept to advocate sanctions that would nudge that government to accept negotiation as the means of breaking the cycle of violence, ending apartheid, and establishing a structure of genuine democracy in South Africa.

Our negotiating concept could still provide a basis for breaking the present deadlock, provided of course that the South African government can diminish what I will call the "confidence gap" they themselves widened by torpedoing our mission at the end of May 1986.

Our negotiating concept, which I am pleased to see has been endorsed in the report of the Secretary of State's Advisory Committee on South Africa, released in January 1987, has four central points:

On the part of the Government:

Removal of the military from the townships, providing for freedom of assembly and discussion and suspension of detention without trial.

The release of Nelson Mandela and other political prisoners and detainees.

The unbanning of the ANC and PAC and the permitting of normal political activity.

On the part of the ANC and others:

Entering negotiations and suspending violence.

In order for such negotiations to succeed, black South Africans will have to set aside their differences. The most detrimental rift is between the ANC and Chief Gatsha Buthelezi's

Inkatha movement, whose support has come largely through an appeal to the Zulu sense of identity. We have seen in Nigeria, however, that political support organized on the basis of ethnicity is detrimental to national unity, and that leaders who encourage such ethnic politics have done great disservice to themselves and their country.

The best chance to create essential black unity in South Africa, including Inkatha, lies in the reconciling role Nelson Mandela can play, once he is released and political activities are allowed. As a result of conversations with him, with Buthelezi, and with others in and outside South Africa, we are certain of this possibility. Such a united front is not likely to be palatable to a South African government wedded to its hitherto successful divide-and-rule policy. But here again trading partners may be able to persuade them that their self-interest lies in such an arrangement. This united front would contain mature, seasoned, responsible leadership that can carry the bulk of the black population with them in orderly and negotiated change.

Among South Africa's major trading partners, only the United States responded to the call in our report for economic measures to induce South Africa to negotiate with authentic black leaders once it had rejected our negotiating concept out of hand. This affirmation of American values and ideals through the bold action of the Congress puts the United States ahead of its allies, thus setting a goal for those allies to achieve. It has also gone some distance in restoring black Africans' shattered confidence in America's commitment to justice, without in any way minimizing the importance of the Comprehensive Anti-Apartheid Act of 1986, there is more to be done.

One program that the United States could sponsor is to assist white South Africans who feel they cannot live with the inevitable change to emigrate and live in other parts of the world of their choice. If some black South Africans similarly so wish and choose, the scheme should not exclude them.

On the issue of sanctions, opponents have always argued that they would not be effective, only serving to drive the Afrikaners deep into the laager. What has since happened in South Africa has not borne out such a view. On the contrary, what we see are cracks in Afrikaner solidarity: not, as before, merely to the right, but for the first time, producing people pressing for more liberal policies. These defections are bound to have significance in the coming elections and beyond, though defeat of the Nationalist Party is not in sight. The government will have to consider formulating policies that take these new pressures into account.

Election or no election, I believe, based on my experience in South Africa, that President P.W. Botha has the authority and the power to bring about the changes necessary. His successor may very well not have such authority for some time, particularly in view of Botha's special relationship with the military. Hence the urgency of increased pressure placed on his government from outside to persuade him to enter into the necessary negotiations, an urgency only made clearer by recent statements suggesting prolonging the state of emergency for as much as two years.

Thus I subscribe to the recommendation set forth by the secretary of state's advisory committee that "The President [should] seize the opportunity created by the passage of the Comprehensive Anti-Apartheid Act of 1986 to take the lead in implementing and publicly communicating a policy toward South Africa that will," among other things, "mobilize other members of the international community in a concerted effort to promote negotiations in South Africa and prevent escalating conflict throughout the region." This, in my view, should begin with pressing America's allies and trading partners to conform with the actions legislated by Congress in fall of 1986.

It is vitally important that economic measures to induce change in South Africa not remain a one-nation affair. Unless the rest of South Africa's trading partners and investors are made to join in the effort, American actions alone may be too little. Coordinated sanctions, combined with coordinated dis-investment that encourages black entrepreneurship and man-agement, constitute the necessary next step.

Indeed, I am gratified that, through the pressure of Con-gress and American public opinion, Israel has now been per-suaded to revise some of its policies of military sales to and cooperation with South Africa. Monitoring must of course continue to assure compliance in this case, as in others.

I want to recognize at this juncture the unparallelled public debate and media coverage of South Africa's human tragedy in the United States. Having travelled much of the globe in the past year in connection with this issue, I know that no other democracy has devoted the same attention and effort to it, and Americans should know that their under-standing and sympathy, and the actions that have flowed from them, have not gone unnoticed on our continent. The challenge of apartheid demands that we keep up the mo-mentum.

Although their understanding of the South African issue is well ahead of that of their allies, Americans do not seem to make the connection between the situation in South Africa and the rest of the region as well as some Europeans do. Un-derlying their empathy for the blacks in South Africa has been their willingness to suspend their all-too-frequent bipolar, ideological judgment of issues and personalities there. Unfor-tunately this entirely appropriate view of Southern Africa's political dynamics lapses when they cross the Limpopo River, South Africa's northern boundary.

South Africa is the hub of economic activity in the region. It draws labor from neighboring countries, it is their major trading partner, and it controls the transportation and com-munications networks on which they have been forced by geography and history to depend. South Africa, which vehe-mently opposes sanctions as an instrument of policy to be applied to itself, vehemently imposes economic sanctions on its neighbors, and effectively too. It not only interferes with the flow of goods, services, and labor; it also prevents the establishment of industry and the development of infrastructure in the most dependent of those countries.

Not satisfied with that, South Africa goes further, launching military incursions into neighboring territories at will. In such a vulnerable situation, all governments in the region will seek assistance wherever they can, with little regard for the ideological complexion of their benefactors. Further, in the cases of especially Angola and Mozambique, which had to fight for their independence, the factors I mentioned in the first chapter come into play: gratitude and reaction against the ideological stance of the colonial power and its allies.

Setting aside Angola for the moment, South Africa's other neighbors in the region deserve greater American consideration than they have received. These countries must be given the wherewithal to become less vulnerable to the economic sanctions tap which South Africa turns on and off at will. But just as South Africa is the major economic engine of the region, so is it also by far the greatest military power. Its neighbors have to be able to defend themselves.

Here the British are playing a very constructive role in Zimbabwe and Mozambique by training their military personnel and organizing their logistic support. It is unlikely that Mrs. Thatcher's government would rush to the support of governments whose feet are set in ideological cement. I know myself at first hand that realities have long since overtaken Prime Minister Mugabe's rhetoric, and it is well known that Mozambique has been making economic overtures to the West for some years. It is time for the United States to join in providing non-lethal military assistance to Mozambique and Zimbabwe. Such an American commitment would serve as an important deterrent to South Africa's military adventurism in the region. So long as Mozambique's security is in jeopardy, so long will the security of Zambia, Zimbabwe, Tanzania, not to mention Botswana and Malawi, be at risk.

The critical factors that link economic issues with security are transportation and communications, in both of which South Africa is almost entirely in control of the region. For Zambia, Zimbabwe, Botswana, and Malawi the transportation network that is both complementary and alternative to South Africa's runs through Mozambique. These countries cannot achieve any significant measure of economic independence and national security without being able to rely with confidence on this alternative.

There are three rail routes to the coast, ending in Maputo, Beira, and Nacala. Of these, the highest priority should be placed on Maputo and Beira. Beira's rehabilitation is already receiving substantial assistance from the Scandinavian countries and Holland; there is no reason why America cannot join in the effort. But receiving less attention, and more important for the economic survival of Botswana, is the Maputo route, which is in even greater disrepair and thus needing American assistance the more.

Fortunately the State Department has successfully resisted pressure on itself and on the Congress to cut aid to Mozambique on ideological grounds and to support a South African-backed insurgency. Yet in view of Mozambique's situation, which has deteriorated from the time that the United States played a crucial role in securing its agreement to the Nkomati Accords with South Africa, the United States should increase its economic assistance. For example, a relatively small amount—say $10 million—would make it possible to bring Mozambique's three cement factories back into production.

There are also viable ventures awaiting foreign capital. Companies disinvesting from South Africa should explore possibilities of investment in Mozambique and other SADCC (Southern Africa Development Coordinating Committee) countries. Indeed, private investment apart, the United States should increase its official development assistance to the countries of the region. It should support SADCC's package of measures to lessen dependence on South Africa, and to strengthen the economies of such countries as Zambia that have vulnerable economies and, further, have paid a heavy price over the years for assisting liberation movements in the region.

Focusing on Zimbabwe now, it is one of Africa's few success stories. Politically, the Constitution agreed to at the Lancaster House talks in 1979–80 remains unchanged, and white Zimbabweans, to their own surprise in some cases, readily acknowledge that they have no problems. Indeed, a number of those who fled to South Africa at the time of independence, are flocking back to find that the most striking change is the considerable appreciation in the value of the property they sold on leaving. They now tell their friends in South Africa that the political problem in Zimbabwe is solved, and they feel more secure returning there than continuing to live in South Africa. Further, a new rapprochement is evolving between the government and opposition parties, which may lead to the kind of one-party democracy I discussed in Chapter 1.

Economic production is on the increase, particularly in agriculture. One can hardly overstate the significance of the fact that, in 1986, Zimbabwe sold a substantial amount of maize to South Africa, thereby demonstrating that the interdependence between South Africa and its neighbors works in both directions. This was possible because Zimbabwe now has a three-year maize surplus, largely the result of the efforts of small holders, who have increased production without displacing the commercial farmers.

But Zimbabwe is now facing both its achievements and difficulties with no assistance from the United States. On the merits of the case, aid, cut off over a trivial diplomatic incident, should be resumed.

Zimbabwe's successes should provide an object-lesson to South Africa's whites. Yet the South African government has taken measures to prevent them from seeing or reading about Zimbabwe's achievements. In fact, the only serious threat to these impressive attainments comes from South Africa's unpredictable use of military and economic weapons against Zimbabwe. It is important to note that despite this threat, exercised several times recently, Zimbabwe has not asked for external military assistance, apart from the British training team. At the same time, Zimbabwe has contributed significantly to secure the Beira Corridor line of transportation and communication within Mozambique.

The longer the intractable problem South Africa continues to pose to the region goes unsolved, the more devastating the consequences, not only for the years just ahead, but for future generations in these countries. UNICEF has recently issued a report detailing the profoundly destructive effect of deprivation and violence on children most of all. We have already seen the impact of the brutalization on the youth in South Africa; no country in the region escapes it. Western countries generally, but America in particular, can be counted upon to respond with admirable concern and generosity to such human tragedy, especially where children are the victims.

Where, however, ideological factors impinge on their understanding of African situations, Americans' vision of what is at stake invariable becomes blurred. This brings me to the U.S. policy toward Angola. In the eyes of Africa, the central security issue that organizes attitudes toward the Angolan situation is South Africa, in the context of the regional destabilization I have been discussing. In contrast, since before Angola's independence, Americans have taken an East-West ideological view of the main issues there. They have gone one step further, going beyond what long-range Soviet design they see in Africa to develop almost a fixation with the role in Angola of the Soviet Union's ally, Cuba.

Thus we have the anomaly of America joining South Africa as the only Western countries that do not recognize the Angolan government. This is difficult for us in Africa to understand, from a country that does maintain relations with other Communist governments, such as the Soviet Union and China. I have come to realize that American domestic political issues play a large role in this; that in fact one could say that the United States has less a policy toward Angola based on that country's African setting than one based on its own domestic politicking.

At a time when the American public scarcely knew the location of Angola, the CIA, as we all know, was working to engineer a government for that independent country that would be in avowedly anti-Marxist hands. We know too that that effort came to a stop in 1976, with passage of the Clark Amendment prohibiting covert American assistance to anti-government forces in Angola. Senator Dick Clark, then Chairman of the Africa Subcommittee of the Senate Foreign Relations Committee, did understand that the invasion by South Africa in November 1975, undertaken with similar aims if not the express endorsement of the Americans, was what threw the support of all Africa behind Angola's Marxist MPLA government.

With the advent of the Carter Administration, we in Nigeria worked closely with, especially Cyrus Vance and Andrew Young, who both took the lead to incorporate an understanding of African views on Southern African issues into American policy and action. Secretary Vance's ability to separate the central issues in Angola from extraneous ones had the Administration actually on the verge of normalizing relations with Angola when his effort was derailed by the intrusion again of American domestic politics, this time in the form of reacting to a supposed Soviet brigade just "discovered" to be in Cuba.

The time has come for the United States to recognize the MPLA government in Angola. An American multinational oil company that has been in Angola since before independence supports such action. A Republican Administration should be willing to listen to such a company.

When changes in the American political scene brought

the repeal of the Clark Amendment nine years later, an even more extreme ideological view came with it. We in Africa found Angola a target of the so-called Reagan Doctrine, with Jonas Savimbi's UNITA movement even supplied with America's sophisticated and portable stinger anti-aircraft missiles. This is the same Administration that will not consider providing non-lethal military assistance to the Frontline states—South Africa's neighbors.

This material support of Jonas Savimbi, trained after all in Peking and widely seen as an opportunist and a stooge of South Africa, has poisoned black African views of America, in South Africa, in the region, and on the continent as a whole. It is in the enlightened self-interest of the United States, as well as in the interest of peace and security in the region, to reverse this policy. I am pleased to see that there is a move to do so already in the Congress.

Let me say a few words about the issue of ideology and this important matter of enlightened self-interest. I do not minimize the importance of the ideological differences, competition, and conflict that dominate relations between the superpowers. Nor do I suggest that there is nothing to choose between ideologies, or that Africa can escape consideration of them and their impact. But what I want to make clear is this: that in view of their colonial past and the long association of Western political and economic institutions with oppression—continuing in the case of South Africa—it cannot be a surprise that Africans have reservations about unequivocal commitment to a Western capitalist camp.

Thus, if the United States and other Western nations wish to encourage leaders of such countries to adhere to their own ideological outlook, they need to be sure not to work at cross-purposes to Africans' most deeply held commitments. We are talking about both liberation and the end of oppression based on race, issues on which Africans cannot compromise.

We have seen elsewhere in Africa that, once those aims

are achieved, African leaders turn to new priorities, largely those of development. We have seen further that the Eastern bloc, though readily contributing military assistance for liberation and strengthening national security, is not so forthcoming with official development assistance. Finally, we can point to a number of cases in Africa which, after an East-leaning start, have for economic reasons moved toward greater cooperation with the West. Mozambique is a striking example.

It is in this sense, then, that I speak as I have of the enlightened self-interest of the United States. I am convinced that, not only in the case of Angola, but in all of Southern Africa including South Africa, it can only benefit America to play a role actively supporting those working to end apartheid and, in the Frontline states, to defend their countries against South African economic and military reprisals.

Thus, once the threat to life and property is ended in Angola, the United States, now recognizing the government, should assist in rehabilitating the Benguela railway, in line with the priority SADCC places on transportation networks. Zambia in particular would then have more reliable means of enhancing its tottering economy.

I have long held the view that there is no place over the long term for foreign troops on the African continent. Thus I too would like to see the departure of Cuba's forces, among others, as soon as possible from Africa. That, of course, requires an atmosphere of security and relative harmony, free from the play of superpower politics and the regional hegemony of apartheid South Africa.

From my conversations with Fidel Castro and José Eduardo dos Santos, I can tell you that they agree that Cuban troops will not remain on Angolan soil a day longer than necessary to protect that country from South African invasions and South African-supported insurgencies. Unfortunately, recent American policy linking the withdrawal of Cuban troops to the issue of Namibian independence has only complicated this prospect.

In recent years any discussion of Angola inevitably brings Namibia along with it. When I was in government in Nigeria, I believed that we had an excellent opportunity to solve the Namibian problem through the process spearheaded by the Carter Administration in conformity with the provisions of United Nations Resolution 435. Since my recent experience in South Africa, however, I have come reluctantly to the conclusion that my belief was an illusion. South Africa will scuttle any such effort, using whatever means are at hand, just as it destroyed the mission of the Eminent Persons Group.

Even at the time of our greatest optimism for a settlement in Namibia, the South African government came with the provision that Walvis Bay, the country's only natural deep-water port, be excised from Namibia and made part of South Africa. With the advent of the Reagan Administration, South Africa latched on to linkage between the withdrawal of Cubans from Angola and Namibia's independence.

Reluctant as Angola was, as a sovereign country, to accept such an external dictation of its security arrangements, if South Africa had been genuine in pulling back from Namibia, and if America had been a truly honest broker, Angola would in its long-range interest have gone further than the phased withdrawal of Cuban troops, which they did accept. What I mean by "truly honest broker" is one willing to exert as much pressure on South Africa as on weaker Angola to comply with agreed arrangements.

Although the Namibian issue should continue to be treated on its own merit, rather than as an appendage of either the Angolan or the South African problems, I believe that a solution may be contingent on change in South Africa itself. This underscores yet again the urgency of accelerating the process that will lead to this change. So long as a fair, just, and humane solution to the South African problem eludes us, for so long will America's policy in Africa run the risk of being received more negatively than positively.

Working out the specifics of that solution must ultimately

lie in the hands of all the people of South Africa themselves. They may wish to avail themselves of the good offices of the international community, which should be ready to respond to their requests, whatever they may be. Undue involvement of outsiders in the process of negotiation is likely to be counterproductive.

With the eradication of apartheid in South Africa, whenever it may come, I see an evolving Southern African region of prosperity and stability, making a contribution to the development of the rest of continent as one of the six confederations of Africa in the twenty-first century.

About the Author

Commissioned into the Nigerian Army in 1959, General Obasanjo served with the United Nations peacekeeping force in the Congo in 1960–61, returning then to Nigeria and a military career that included leading the division that put an end to the Nigerian Civil War in January 1970. Commander of the Nigerian Army Engineering Corps from 1970 to 1975, he went on to serve as Federal Commissioner for Works and Housing. Head of State of Nigeria from 1976 to 1979, he presided over the carefully executed transition to civilian democratic rule in that year.

Turning his attention to farming after his retirement from government and the army, he set out to demonstrate by personal example the importance of agriculture to African development and stability. At the same time, he has continued to address critical international issues, notably through his membership in the Independent Commission on Disarmament and Security Issues (the Palme Commission); in the InterAction Council of Former Heads of Government and its executive committee; as co-chairman of the Commonwealth Eminent Persons Group on Southern Africa; and as a member of the United Nations panel of Eminent Persons on the Relationship between Disarmament and Development.